In the Canyons of Despair

Keith Seddon

This essay connects the author's experience of current affairs to his personal story of grief, attempting a fusing of the autobiographical with the polemical and political.

It places personal despair into a global context of political manipulation to which we are all subject, whether its victims are aware of it or not, drawing on the work of documentary film-maker Adam Curtis as its impetus.

KEITH SEDDON was born in London in 1956. In the 1980s, at Hatfield Polytechnic and at University College London, he pursued his interests in the humanities and philosophy, acquiring his PhD (addressing the metaphysics of time) in 1986, after which he worked as an educator, tutor, and associate lecturer in a wide variety of contexts, at all levels of further and higher education. His wife of 37 years, Jocelyn Almond, for whom he had been her full-time carer, died in 2014. He lives in Hertfordshire, England, where he makes Anglo-Saxon lyres and composes music for the instrument. He is currently completing a translation of the Middle English Christian mystical writings of Julian of Norwich and recording notes on the philosophy of pessimism.

In the Canyons of Despair

Oh-dearism and the nightmare
of non-linear politics

Keith Seddon

SWAYING WILLOW PRESS

First published 2017 by Swaying Willow Press

BM BOX 1129, LONDON, WC1N 3XX

Book & Typographical Design by Keith Seddon
Typeset in Rival 10 pt.

Printed by CreateSpace

ISBN 978-1-5450-4988-4 (paperback)

The power of accurate observation is commonly called cynicism by those who have not got it.

GEORGE BERNARD SHAW

1

SOMETIMES I SIT as still as I can, unmoving, hardly breathing at all, in little, shallow gasps, like someone hiding in the ruins from the sniper's aim, desperate, so desperate not to move. For these are moments when the whole of life seems nothing but bullets and things collapsing, when all thought of effort serves to establish all the more irrevocably the uselessness of all action, the hopelessness of all hope. As one may sit and wait for the sniper to grow bored or conclude his vigil with the need to relieve himself, so I too wait, unmoving.

———————

And in such moments swells my awareness that so much seems to be so terribly wrong. All is in crisis, perpetual crisis. Propelled onwards by ineffectual constraints, global warming *runs on unchecked*. A new species extinction event is proceeding so rapidly that *hardly anyone notices*. Crooks, lunatics, madmen and narcissists are in charge, and they all seem to be wearing the face of the Joker in the Batman stories. This sense of wrongness is not unique to my personal story, for it courses down through every layer of being, in every nation, every institution, every enterprise and, eventually, right at its very depths, it cleaves through each individual's psyche, and is so effective in its destruction that, like the best adapted parasites, it numbs any awareness to its presence in almost all those it afflicts. It works its evil in legion ways, and beguiles its victims into proceeding as willing hosts. It whispers seductively, 'Keep calm and carry on,' and even entices its host to pin up a poster to that effect in the hallway or kitchen, or to upload a meme to Facebook.

2

THROUGH LUMINOUS CANYONS of concrete and glass I see from the omnibus the populace of the city groping its weary way along sweltering pavements. Each exhausted soul is silent for the most part, solitary for the most part, glancing up occasionally; each weighed down by something, or else pulling after them sluggish sledges stacked with regrets and setbacks that had become surgically attached to them years ago. No joy this day in these dismal, bright streets, just drudgery and the same old

---

routine, the same old static faces worn out by sameness, sad with sorrows unresolved.

The omnibus had arrived at roadworks and had not moved for ten minutes, so the driver opened the doors to let out the unbearable heat and permit a brief, refreshing breeze to relieve for a moment the thickening oppression. Deciding to get off, yanking at my own sledge, I joined the dismal throng and headed towards my own unknown terminus. I mean *unknown* in the sense that I cannot now remember the purpose of my journey, because there is no regular routine to which my memory may attach, as I do not live in London but in one of its satellite towns whose proximity makes day trips possible, if a little expensive. Perhaps the British Museum had beckoned. Perhaps this was the day that I marvelled at how small the ancient Greek helmets were in a large display cabinet in the long Enlightenment Gallery, forcing the conclusion that the people who had worn them, those who had died wearing them and those who would die later on wearing them again, and even those who had died of something entirely non-battle related, *must have had extremely small heads.* These helmets would have been a tight fit on a chimpanzee or a child, and I could not help but visualise myself on the ancient battlefield, towering over all the soldiers who, *down there,* two feet lower than me at a different altitude, were wielding diminutive spears and swords and screaming their rage and pain in little high-pitched voices, and falling hardly any distance at all when the fatal blow came down to smash open the gash in the bronze helmet whose provenance now brings it here, these few thousand years later, to this cabinet, in this museum. Or perhaps I had come to look at books in a bookshop, or guitars in a guitar shop.

And I cannot remember on account of a more significant and a more interesting reason, because as I stepped down from the bus and eased myself into the plodding flow of pedestrians, it took hardly three seconds for me to trip over two thoughts. The first was quite a big thought, perhaps half-way along the Scale of How Big Thoughts Are, for it had reached that point that counts as an insight, the recalling or recovering or realising of something that you have never thought before, or had had no occasion to think about for a very long time, or quite in this way, revealing some significant idea that changes the way something is understood. It was a long and convoluted thought, the sort that needs to be carefully mapped out if it is going to make any sense or be of any use, be that for the thinker themselves or for mere onlookers.

My dear wife had died roughly 18 months

previously, and the bleakness of the world that her loss provoked had not diminished or even thinned a little or become a touch more fuzzy round the edges. The reverse was happening. The passing of the days since she had passed, their numerical expansion, was increasing the bleakness which, for all this time, had lain at the centre of everything. It had formed itself, all those months before, into the molten, dense core of my being, unmovable, radiating a sort of paralysis, an unbearable taste of wrongness that flavoured time itself … it was at the core of all my thoughts, of every thought I had had since that fateful night. So all was done and everything happened in the context of my loss. For instance, I did not simply read a book, but I read it as someone who was perpetually aware that he would never again be able to introduce some remarks about it – about this book or any other – into a conversation with the person who mattered most. And it seemed that I had all of a sudden become aware of similar molten cores at the centres of so many others, who one way or another – because this is of course the way of the world – had suffered some unbearable catastrophe or loss or disappointment of one sort or another, and through the impetus of their own cores' malignant radiation they had at some point been projected into a world that was now different, where nothing made proper sense, just like me ... we were Brothers and Sisters in the Order of the Molten Core.

That was (in large part) the character of the sledge that I pulled behind me as I stepped off the bus into the bright canyon of that London street on that hot, hot day.

She had been disabled all her adult life from the age of 25, struck down into a way of living circumscribed by an iron wall of progressively worsening immobility that thickened and tightened with evermore intensity such that for the last 15 years she could sit only if the chair supported her, though could still hold small books and a spoon (not at the same time) if I brought them to her, and which inhibited all trips beyond our little house saving only infrequent medical appointments at nearby locations. Because of this utter confinement, we tried to look beyond, as may a prisoner confined to a bleak cell who can climb up to gape through his bars at another world and see trees and the sky and perhaps distant sails, or kites being flown by children, so we would watch the television. We devoured all we could manage: history, the natural world, science, politics and current affairs, but especially anything idiosyncratic, anything quirky, anything that would blow the refreshing breeze of novelty or innovation over us. This is why she would have so loved Jonathan Pie, whom she never saw, because he did not exist in those days, and why we watched Charlie Brooker's satirical, sarcastic and acerbic news reviews. Perhaps he was the only one at that time who reflected the world back to us – the world of politics and current affairs, of pretence and deceit – in the drab colours in which we saw it ourselves, in a tone that contained our anger and frustration and disquiet and comforted us with the message that we were not alone in finding this world disturbing, distressing, disorienting, disordered and deranged. And that is why on the evening of 8 April 2009 we watched the third episode of Brooker's new news review, *Newswipe*, which contained a five-minute contribution by the documentary film-maker Adam Curtis about a new psychological disorder that was spreading through populations worldwide, a new disease caused by watching television news.

Curtis tells us that television news is often

perceived to be boring, because it is often about politics, which can be very dull (and from the 1970s, I am guessing, he offers a hilariously apt illustration of this concerning government grants to Scottish coal mines), but it can also be about *something else*, much more disturbing than a dose of intolerable dullness could ever be. The problem with watching television news is that, night after night, we are shown pictures of terrible, terrible things that we feel we can do nothing about: pictures of civil wars, massacres and starving children and, more recently we may also add, images of refugees fleeing death and destruction, sometimes wading ashore with tiny bundles that represent a whole life's achievement whilst, somewhere behind them, further up the beach or on a different island, someone has discovered the little corpse of a child resting in the gently lapping waves, an entirely innocent soul not deprived of their life's possessions, but deprived of life itself. And in response to such images, all we can do in our powerlessness is utter the words 'Oh dear.' This condition, Curtis tells us, is called *oh-dearism*.

And in that moment the deadly serious collides with the absurd, highlighting, all the more effectively (if I may extend the account that Curtis offers) that something must be terribly, terribly wrong with human affairs – if not more wrong than they have ever been, more wrong in the sense that we today, all of us, have had foisted upon us through television news a new consciousness of our condition at the same time as being aware that civilisation (if we dare use that term) has never before been so technically capable of solving any problem that might arise. This is all the more keenly felt because we see around us examples of problems that have indeed been solved by technical ingenuity: from the spread of renewable energy and the ubiquitous presence of microelectronics in our phones, tablets and other devices, to the spectacle of massive civil engineering projects; from the wonder of organ transplants, cochlear implants, and steady progress on developing cures for cancer, to the innovations required for smart, environmentally efficient buildings; from developments in agriculture to developments in satellite technology. There seems to be no practical limit to what technical ingenuity might accomplish, no impediment to the solving of any problem if only there were to be a sufficient political will to bring it about. And that means there need be no suffering for anyone, anywhere ... certainly no need for any lack of medical provision, no need for lack of housing or effective sanitation, no need for any lack of education. Any and each deprivation is prolonged as a political choice not to put in place

---

the technical solutions that would diminish and soon enough remove that deprivation.

Oh-dearism, then, is the condition of feeling helpless and depressed as an inevitable conse-quence of watching television news, and Curtis tells the story of the rise of oh-dearism in his satirically short documentary.

3

I AM OLD ENOUGH to have witnessed the events of the 1960s that would culminate all these years later in the spread of oh-dearism. It all started with the rise of the hippy countercul-ture, whose beginning coincides roughly with the Beatles' mini-tour of Germany in the sum-mer of 1966 when the world was introduced to John Lennon's *Nowhere Man* (released in December 1965 on their album *Rubber Soul*), the portrayal of whom represented a new con-sciousness (not the only one, and one mildly ridiculed by the song) typical of the era, or what

---

would become more typical, possessed by the individual who 'turns on, tunes in and drops out' (words coined by, or perhaps just promoted by Timothy Leary near enough at the same time that the Beatles were on stage in Germany), and who cultivates a certain detachment from the madness of the world, substituting for that madness a sort of hedonism championed by altered states of consciousness and individual expression. This has of course been mocked mercilessly in its outward manifestations of painting flowers onto Volkswagen camper vans, wearing ridiculously wide trousers (but wide only from the knee down) and eating lentils. The impetus for this mockery stems mostly, as I recall, from the panic induced by hippies in those privileged enough to occupy positions of power and authority within the Establishment, or otherwise wedded to the status quo and the little bit of power that they may have wielded

---

from within the narrow circuits of their own lives which were of course no less than anyone else's also circumscribed by the institutions they wanted to conserve and promote.

4

AND THAT IS WHY Curtis remarks in his film that the story of the rise of oh-dearism in television news began when radicals within the emerging counterculture of the 1960s embraced the (now so blindingly obvious) insight that all politics is corrupt because it always involves power. Could the radicals bypass politicians and find a new way to connect directly with those dispossessed and suffering? In 1968, western politicians proved themselves power-less in finding solutions to the humanitarian crisis caused by the Biafran Civil War in West-

———

ern Africa. Here were images of starving children, yet radicals, celebrities and others offered ways in which we, the viewers, could assert our own power to influence affairs. Prominent through the little hole at the end of the Kaleidoscope of History is the BBC's *Blue Peter Appeal* on children's television where they asked their audience to send in parcels of cotton or woollen fabric, garments, blankets, scraps, or even loose thread. They had hoped to reach a target of 144,000 parcels, but were actually sent ten times that quantity, receiving in total an astonishing 1,440,000 parcels. Thus, international aid agencies were indeed able to bypass politics and organise direct international humanitarian relief to those starving in Biafra.

What *Blue Peter* had begun reached its high point with *Live Aid* in July 1985 after reporter Michael Buerk's news footage shocked television audiences with images of the starving

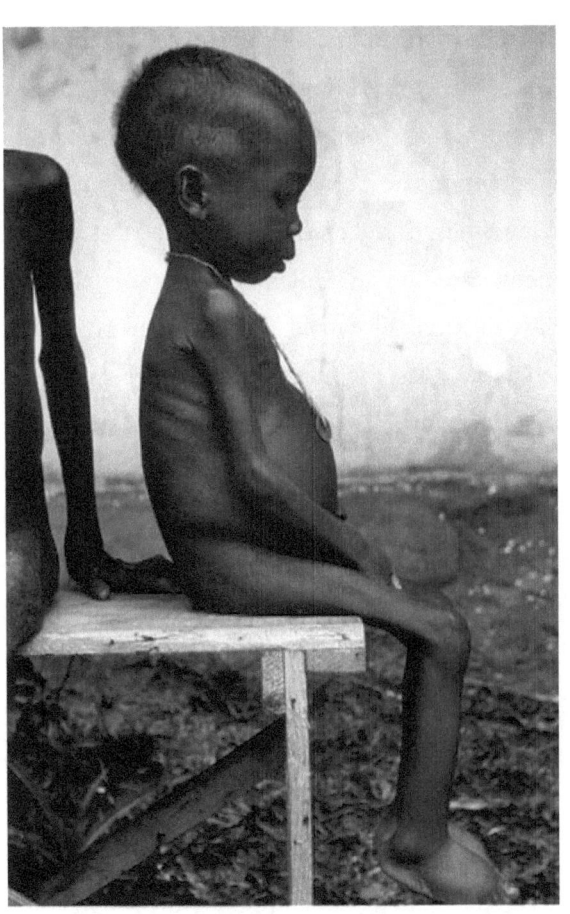

masses in the midst of Ethiopia's appalling famine. Bob Geldof's *Live Aid* events, which saw musicians and singers famous in the world of popular music perform to audiences in Wembley Stadium in London and at the John F. Kennedy Stadium in Philadelphia, were televised live around the world. Revenue for *Live Aid's* charitable endeavours was therefore raised directly from ticket sales, but more significantly was raised from television audiences globally, by getting them to phone in to make altruistic donations using their credit cards and thereby securing the support of millions (the BBC in the UK manned 300 telephone lines to take payments). This event established with stunning clarity what had already been shown all those years before by *Blue Peter*, that ordinary people, *that we*, working collectively, could do more to bring needed change to the world than could our corrupted politicians. It is estimated that a global audience of 1.9 billion, across 150 nations, watched the live broadcasts, raising a sum in total of £150m, entirely bypassing all and any political procedure, and in the process made us feel good about ourselves. We had been altruistic and marvellously munificent, and at the same time had recognised something that surely overwhelmed any lingering, paralysing helplessness, as, undeniably, those in Ethiopia who had received food aid that otherwise would not have come to them were undoubtedly helped and their plight relieved. But what was the real cost of this munificence? In attempting to transcend the corruption of politics, *Live Aid* probably sent our money, some of our money, unwittingly to be sure, to accounts controlled by Ethiopia's corrupt leader, dictator Colonel Mengistu, from where he could fund the civil war he was fighting, prolonging it by a further six years, causing as many deaths (conjectured *Médecins Sans Frontières*) as had been saved by the food relief. Mengistu may even have diverted food aid directly to his soldiers. None of this was reported, because it was too complicated and would have taken the glow off our self-satisfying generosity. I remember some few years later watching a documentary with my wife which explained, contrary to received opinion, that the Ethiopian famine did not result from drought, certainly not entirely from drought, but was caused by the deliberate tactic of destroying crops and farmland as a strategy against one's enemies and aggravated by the Ethiopian government's enforced resettlement programmes, employed as part of its counter-insurgency efforts. The whole thing was pretty much a scam, and corruption had not been by-passed at all, but had been supported and enabled. Oh dear ...

Then, in 1989, the Berlin Wall came down

and the west won the cold war. The old political story of left versus right, that had served so well from the end of the second world war, by which events were managed and interpreted, could no longer be used, and the news needed a new all-encompassing and simple story to account for events. And the story which took its place came rushing from the *Blue Peter* studio and the *Live Aid* arenas to save the day. The Kaleidoscope of Current Affairs was turned and twizzled until the old counterculture story that had explained the Biafran and Ethiopian famines came into focus, and world affairs – 'all the chaotic events and fragments of stuff that happen every day', as Curtis calls the news – were from this point explained in terms of 'the struggle between innocent individuals and corrupt political systems'. And it worked. What would otherwise be a stream of disordered and unrelated events illuminating our television screens, by applying this substitute story of How the World Works, now made perfect sense of it all, removing the chaos and replacing it with a narrative that put everything in order. The fall of communist regimes in Eastern Europe, the student uprising in Tiananmen Square, the horrors of the Bosnian War, the Siege of Sarajevo and the Srebrenica massacre could be made to make perfect sense when reported, as Curtis remarks, from within the story of 'noble individuals bravely standing up against bad political systems'.

Until, that is, the story of good versus evil that made sense of the news stopped making sense of the news, which happened in 1994 with the Rwandan genocide when a million Tutsis were killed by Hutus, causing millions of Tutsis to flee as refugees and flood into neighbouring Congo. Flooding in with them came western aid workers, ready to help the innocent victims, and western journalists ready to tell a new story of innocent good people versus blame-worthy evil people. But when it became apparent that sneaking into the refugee camps together with the innocent Tutsis came also evil Hutus who had participated in the genocide, whose discovery on the part of Tutsis resulted in more Tutsis coming from Rwanda with the express purpose of invading the camps and murdering their murderers to get revenge, the story of good versus evil by which the news sought to explain the news obviously made no sense, for now it appeared that the innocent Tutsis were also prepared to indulge in mass killing, precipitating further conflict in which over subsequent years a further four and a half million people died. Everyone was evil, and in the absence of a story that could explain events, events could not be explained, and all we were left with was a bunch of evil people and another bunch of evil people all doing evil things that made no sense and defied all understanding. We saw footage of little children struggling to hold up massive automatic rifles, so even the children were evil.

In the absence of news that reported such terrible events in terms of political struggle, and with the failure of the good versus evil narrative, television news portrayed events as inherently disordered, occurring randomly, chaotically, adrift from any coherent analysis of why any of this was happening. Global affairs, therefore, served to fuel the only plausible account for why all the fragments of stuff kept on happening, and that was that human beings as a species were inherently evil, and human nature itself was corrupted and would always and inevitably lead to cruelty and suffering for which there could never be any remedy, and to which the only response was 'Oh dear'.

5

ON THAT HOT DAY, as I dragged my sledge away from the bus, all those dreary faces in a moment of insight connected like a spark completing an electrical circuit to Adam Curtis's new psychological disease of *oh-dearism*, and suddenly each and every face manifested this condition of hopeless depression. And then a second thought quickly followed, for the insight spoke of another layer, revealing something extra: it is not just the television news which induces oh-dearism, but the events we directly experience, for some of us, some of the time,

---

from within the folly of our own lives. Marx would have said it. He would have said that the alienation he had noticed, the detachment that every working person experiences when the economic system itself sunders each of them from the product of their own labour, induces oh-dearism, the hopeless and paralysing depression that manifests in an overwhelming sense of powerlessness, of being subject to events without really being a part of them, and certainly not having any kind of role in shaping them, and certainly not within the workplace, not unless you are an owner or a major share-holder. And for those of us who are aware of how far down oh-dearism keeps us submerged in the gloom of despair, we may bring forward a single, feeble thought that the severity of the evil inflicted upon others has not yet come to our own door. Perhaps we feel justified in thinking that such evil could never approach us

---

as closely as it approaches others. Otherwise we must admit the discomforting idea, under-mining this rickety excursion towards some minimal consolation, that it is perhaps only a matter of time, only a matter of waiting for the narcissists and bigots to come to power, only a matter of waiting for agreement and concilia-tion to be eroded by fear and stupidity, until the worst of all evils, whatever character it may prove to have for our own personal stories, catches up with us and we fall under its swip-ing, mindless, moronic claws. Then we too will end up – one way or another, metaphorically or literally – being caressed by gentle waves on a beach we do not know, beyond which will be no life at all, or a life we do not want and cannot control or manage ... a life whose living seems pointless and without merit.

For some few minutes the pavement seemed to sway under my feet. My sudden diagnosis of oh-dearism in everyone around me and in myself had provoked an awareness of specific symptoms, of a sense of terrible instability, of finding that what should be pleasant (I was off to the museum, or a bookshop, or somewhere *nice*, after all) was now abruptly *unpleasant*. It was as if, given my grief and unbearable sadness, aware now of living in the presence of everyone else's sadness and in the presence of so much evil embodied in all the fragments of stuff that just kept on happening, nothing interesting, nothing agreeable would ever again relieve this painful tension that stretched tight the cord between me and my sledge, never again make anything seem worthwhile let alone actually *be worthwhile*. And whether they knew it themselves or not, I could see in the faces of everyone around me the same malaise of sad disappointment, of the inevitability of suffering and powerlessness.

———

And at some point in the days after, in a moment of idle reflection as I sat alone bereft of even sufficient energy to read a book or fight evil on Facebook, I drifted into a waking dream that comes upon me every once in a while.

Waves – Crashing

Imprisoned on this salty shore
Where, in my dreams I bide, I cast a stare
To distant star and sigh in my despair.
Did ever sun rise on this lonely strand?
Or was it always twilight here?
I hear the sounds of surf that surges
Up the shingle and the mounting gale
That starts to shred the leaves of palms
That block my way behind.

I stand and wait and hope to see
A light no star has shed on me,

———

But comes instead from far off lantern
Swinging on a line, on a boat,
Far out to sea.
For that must mean my friend
Has come, a friend I do not know,
Who somehow sees my desperate plight,
So comes to rescue me.

And were I on a boat of mine,
Upon those fateful seas,
I too would sail a course
In hope of finding souls to save.
But, as before, no lantern shines,
No friend will come this time.

The same shore waits for further dreams,
When despair will prod my hope to stir,
And I will stare across the waves,
And hope again in vain.

———

6

AND I REMEMBERED the sad faces I had seen and the unspoken and unrecognised, largely unrecognised, fellowship that binds us in our common plight. The world need not be like this. Those who know better should stand against the oh-dearism that the news promotes. They should be fighting it. They should invade the news and give it a proper thrashing. They should – because they know better – *show us something better*, show us some hope for a future that makes sense and which we want and which it is possible to work for. Are they there,

---

somewhere, working in the shadows perhaps? Because I cannot see them. All is contention and disruption and Labour doing the opposite of what it was founded to do, and instead striving like someone half demented to maintain the status quo of capitalist exploitation whilst oh-dearism and zero-hours contracts work their malicious destruction. The economy grows, yet so do misery and frustration and the prevalence of food banks and the desperation of those compelled to go and beg at their doors, while the success of the economy is transferred to only the wealthy few and to those with power. So contempt also grows: the contempt that those with entitlement feel for everyone else, for their constituents, for their workforces, for paupers especially; the contempt that flows in the opposite direction also grows, the contempt that paupers have for their betters, that constituents have for those who are supposed to represent them, but do not, and instead represent themselves, their friends and families and their own entitled class, and get the paupers, through their VAT payments for lavatory rolls and suchlike, to pay for their duck houses or for heating their stables.

And then the truth dawns, on that hot day, or later bit by bit, the awful and half-unhinged truth dawns that oh-dearism is being promoted deliberately. The television news is not a force of nature that has the character that it happens to have because of the laws of physics or chemistry. It is the manifestation of a policy to manipulate its viewers in this specific way, to deliberately make the world inexplicable and bewildering, to show us that we have power sufficient to change *nothing.* We have been had big time. Point your Kaleidoscope of Current Affairs into a mirror and stare into it; stare and stare, and there amidst all the swirling fragments of stuff, you will eventually see yourself rendered as a puppet whose strings are being pulled and yanked. This is so. The world is so. All is so because those with power have chosen to make it so.

How best to fashion a populace politically impotent? How best to make one's power unassailable and permanent? You bring despair down upon people in such measure and with such a weight of care and apprehension for the future that they are incapable even of comprehending what has happened to them. They do not even see themselves as victims of the system but, in rare moments when a little flicker of energy flows, they will tell you how one day they too will be millionaires, and they too will be able to employ people on minimum wage zero-hours contracts, and live well, oh so well, on the backs of others. Then they will have to start the night shift, or look anxiously through

———

their messages to see if they have been sum-
moned to work or not, and they will forget their
moment of ridiculous grandeur and go back to
being oppressed, yet not realise that this is
what has happened.

I had thought that events generally, that my
bereavement and a bad dose of oh-dearism, had
been manipulating me, casting the world in
these strange hues and casting me always down
into this despair of ever hoping for anything
better. But more importantly for a proper
analysis, a proper grasping for the truth, came
the realisation that the common bond of oh-
dearism which binds all of us, all over the
world, into a paralysing despair, was being deliberately inflicted. It was time to check out the
Internet, and find the documentary that Adam
Curtis had made for Charlie Brooker's review,
and finding it I found that I had remembered its
general drift really very well: it had registered

with my unconscious memory all those years
before and had lain dormant, ready to trigger
that insight on that London pavement on that
hot day. But hold on, here's something that did
not register, something seemingly completely
forgotten. *Curtis had made a second mini-documentary.* I had seen it, and forgotten it because
it had been broadcast at the end of December
2014, only a few weeks after my dear wife had
died. Perhaps it had been forgotten because the
usual routine had been shattered, the routine
we had followed for those few decades of talking and talking, of talking about anything that
appealed to us, about anything that we could
glimpse and take an interest in seen through the
bars from within our confining cell of illness
and disability. I assume that is why I had
remembered Curtis's first mini-documentary;
we had rehearsed it, remembered our own direct recollections of the *Blue Peter* broadcast we

had both witnessed whilst we were yet children, unknown to each other. And we remembered getting up early enough (oh my, how getting up for anything, burdened by the require-
ments of illness and disability, had been so very
trying) so as not to miss any of the *Live Aid*
broadcast from Wembley Stadium, of recoiling
slightly when Geldof in his frustration at seeing
how meagre were the donations coming in had
used the F-word, of phoning in with our own
contribution. The second documentary had not
registered because nothing had happened to
wire it into my neural net of memory and
experience. So, thank you, Internet – someone
had put it up on YouTube. And reviewing it
again, I see a near seamless continuation from
the first little film: so do please view them both,
in the right order.

Perhaps, after all, an unconscious memory,
feeble and unformed, had been feeding my

thoughts, for here was Curtis remarking that yes, oh-dearism was deliberately being inflicted on the global television news audience, purposefully deployed as a means of control on the part of those with power, in power, eager to use their power to dominate events *and to dominate us*, the moving components that constitute the very machinery of those events, *whose effective conditioning is required for the schemes of power to prevail.*

7

THIS SECOND SHORT FILM tells the story of Vladislav Surkov, one of Vladimir Putin's key advisors who has helped Putin maintain and retain his power since 1999, who has fulfilled his role in a strange and unique way, bringing ideas from his earlier, short foray into avant-garde art into the world of politics. Surkov has set about undermining people's perception of the world so that it becomes impossible to be certain about what is really happening, and he is doing this not by addressing people directly or influencing their perception at the point perception takes place, but by doing something somewhat simpler, by changing, manipulating and contributing directly to what those perceptions range over: events themselves. Russian politics has been changed by Surkov into a bizarre piece of avant-garde theatre, constantly confusing, unstable, unpredictable and disorienting. Under his direction, Russian society has come to resemble a reality television show that is capricious and disturbing. He has sponsored groups from across the political spectrum, from neo-Nazis on the one hand to liberal human rights campaigners on the other, and where necessary he has facilitated the creation of political groups that he wanted to back. He has even promoted parties opposed to Vladimir Putin. His aim has been to destabilise Russian politics and render it chaotic and frightening. He even willingly admits that this is what he is doing, because doing so guarantees that no one

---

can be certain any more about what is real and what is fake. This is a strategy of power that keeps any opposition on the back foot, never sure that what they are opposing is real or imaginary, a product of Putin's advisors or a product of his enemies.

And against this background of never-ceasing, chaotic confusion, Putin is the only stabilis-

ing force that can prevent a catastrophic de-
scent into Total Chaos. As Russian politics becomes more chaotic and confusing, more power
accrues to President Putin, because there is no
one else to defend the people against the chaos.
Anybody else or any other party that may at-
tempt to offer the required stability may be a

---

fake, created by Surkov, and therefore cannot be trusted.

In March 2014, under his pseudonym Natan Dubovitsky, Surkov published a short story in the magazine *Russky Pioneer*, 'Without Sky', set in the future, after the 'fifth world war', in which Surkov introduces the concept of 'non-linear war'. Unlike a traditional war where we see two clearly defined parties, each opposed to the other, each with its own clear and easily understood agenda, non-linear war is the opposite, in which there are multiple enemies, multiple and ever-changing alliances, and objectives that are never clearly defined, never adhered to for long, and may not even be part of any traditionally understood military objective. Any one party can never properly grasp what any of the others is really trying to do, so strategies for defence become futile, whilst offensive strategies have no clear aims. Non-linear war is not meant to be won, but is conducted as an on-going process, as something permanent and unstoppable. This is the sort of war that George Orwell envisaged in his novel *1984*, a permanent political solution that answers the question of how the people can be managed and controlled. It makes any political opposition essentially treasonable, because only the ruling party has the capacity to fight the endless war. Political opposition is thus incapacitated.

British troops have returned from Afghanistan, but no one can determine whether they won a victory or suffered a defeat. The Americans are fighting their unending, non-linear War on Terror, but no one can say whether they are winning it or not, nor whether it will ever end. This matches Surkov's description of non-linear war, and appears purposefully designed not to end, because its never ending suits the political agenda of those in power and those with power, in the political and economic are-nas. The devastating debacle in Syria may go down in history as the first non-linear war in which alliances and objectives make no coher-ent sense because each party has a different goal and a different understanding of how those other parties relate to, oppose or contrib-ute to their own individual aims.

And seen in the light of non-linear pro-cesses, here in the UK, only the ruling party of our time, the Conservatives, have the motive, intention and capability of reducing the deficit. Austerity is the only policy that can prevail against this awful problem, they tell us. What-ever harms are produced by austerity, what-ever the suffering – we are informed – is justi-fied simply because the objective of reducing the deficit is justified. Yet despite the govern-ment telling us that the deficit is being reduced, it is not; they are lying to us (the national debt now stands at over £1,800bn; it was only £850bn when the Tories came to power in 2010). In order to manipulate the electorate into supporting policies that will harm the general population but benefit the tiny rich elite right at the top, they are lying to us. And people believe them. This is perhaps a more sophisticated version of Surkov's fakery. In Russia, he has had to create actual, if fake, political parties in order to manufacture the enemy of chaos for Putin to champion. In the UK, the government has only had to manipulate an ignorant electorate about how macroeconomics works – laughably false when you look into it – in order to declare themselves the only party capable of solving this problem which is not actually a problem at all. This is the beginning of non-linear politics, in which problems and enemies are deliberately manufactured in order for those in power to declare themselves the only party that can re-

---

store normality. Yet to retain power they do not restore normality, but instead maintain and feed the chaos they claim to be fighting in order to justify their hold on power.

But what is this power for? Whom does it serve? The results of austerity do not serve the children of the homeless families now living in temporary accommodation, and neither did they serve the homeless person who died of hypothermia at the back of a supermarket car park. Austerity does not help those in need of social care that local authorities can no longer afford because of government cutbacks.

While the government has worked hard to take money *out of the economy* under the guise of austerity, it has been working no less hard to pump money *into the economy* in the form of quantitative easing – the equivalent of £24,000 for every family in Britain, Curtis tells us (and that figure relates to 2014, don't forget). Many of those billions (according to the Bank of England) have not gone where they were intended, but have ended up in the pockets of the richest 5%. This represents the largest transfer of wealth *to the rich* in modern times.

8

OH DEAR, OH DEAR. Such a sense of being overwhelmed by the evil that keeps pouring out of the fragments of stuff ... everyday more stupid stuff ... narcissistic, misogynous buffoons voted to the highest office, delivery lorries and cars used as the poor man's weapon of mass destruction, refugees blamed for the actions of terrorists, guards removed from trains because profit is more important than the safety of passengers. And our powerlessness seems overwhelming. Curtis is right when he concludes his second short film saying that in this new, non-linear politics these incoherent, ridiculous events cannot be explained or accounted for by any form of coherent narrative, and therefore opposition is impossible since any would-be opposition cannot even say in clear and meaningful terms what it wishes to oppose.

Oh dear, oh dear, oh dear. Worst of all is this awful sense of not really understanding things (all that 'analysis' above suddenly seems like complete nonsense), yet feeling certain that some particular juxtaposition of ideas and concepts of power, or ideas that for instance address the rise of the right and the demeaning treatment of paupers would make sense of it all. Suddenly everything would fall into place, like tipping out the pieces of a jigsaw puzzle all over the table and finding that miraculously each piece falls exactly where it needs to go for the picture in a second to complete itself and ap-

---

pear whole, all present and correct, and make sense.

My dear wife could do that, she could make sense of things. I've never known such creative intelligence. In her presence, the horrors of the chaotic world were tamed by explanations and interpretations, but also by plans and solutions that eased the fear. She did not suffer from oh-dearism because she understood why things happen as they do. The causes of everything were right there for her, like helmets or other things displayed in a cabinet. But now I no longer hear her calming voice. I am no longer soothed by her revealing explanations in those long, long conversations, and the sickness of oh-dearism has me firmly in its grip. All seems lost and corrupted. The knowledge of the home-less man who died in the cold hurt me as if he had been known to me, and the thought of it still brings tears to my eyes. Why is not everyone affected like that? She would have explained that to me. She would have made sense of the whole sorry saga and eased the pain of this oh-dearism. But now, in my particular story, there can be no more conversations; no more watching the television as we used to do for interesting things, such interesting things. Such a sense of paralysis and hopelessness. So I remain lost and trapped on that dreary beach where day never comes, and where in my waking dreams I retreat to a little ramshackle hut I have fashioned from driftwood under the palms at the back of the roaring shingle, where I sit, oh so still, trying not to breathe, waiting for something I cannot fathom or describe, but which does not come.

PICTURE CREDITS

The 'Keep Calm' poster was devised in 1939 by the British government (but never widely distributed), intended to boost morale in the event of a German invasion and we may conjecture – upon its discovery by German High Command – contributed directly to Hitler's decision not to invade. A population prepared to pin up this particular poster was clearly going to cause a great deal of trouble. This image is in the public domain.

The photograph of the Spartan helmet shows an exhibit on display in the British Museum, sourced from Wikimedia Commons and used under the terms of the Creative Commons Attribution-Share Alike 2.0 Generic License.

The photograph of the sad woman by Jamie Rodriguez is sourced from morguefile.com, a resource that licenses commercial and non-commercial use.

The photograph of the seated, malnourished child taken in a Nigerian relief camp during the Nigerian–Biafran war in the late 1960s is a public domain image sourced from Wikimedia Commons, made available by the Centers for Disease Control and Prevention, Atlanta, Georgia, USA.

———

The photograph of sky between tall buildings is by Jimmy Chang, and the photograph of crashing waves pounding rocks is by Anton Repponen, available from unsplash.com, a resource for photographs that may be used both privately and commercially under the Creative Commons Zero license.

The pictures of Vladislav Surkov and Vladimir Putin are sourced via Wikimedia Commons and are used under Creative Commons Attribution Unported licenses.

TYPEFACE

The text is set in Rival 10 point, designed by the Mostardesign Type Foundary. Rival is a modern serif font family inspired by characters drawn with a round nib. It has many distinctive signs such as broken curves, slightly curved down strokes, curved diagonals, and curved, slanted axes. All these typographic tokens give Rival a modern and contemporary aspect for all kinds of graphic projects.

Available from
youworkforthem.com